AMERICAN SPECIAL OPS

SWAT TEAMS
The Missions

by Robert Grayson

Consultant:
Professor Christian Dobratz
Department of Government,
Law Enforcement Program
Minnesota State University, Mankato

CAPSTONE PRESS
a capstone imprint

Velocity Books are published by Capstone Press,
1710 Roe Crest Drive, North Mankato, Minnesota 56003
www.capstonepub.com

Library of Congress Cataloging-in-Publication Data
Grayson, Robert, 1951–
SWAT teams : the missions / By Robert Grayson.
pages cm.—(Velocity : American special ops)
Includes bibliographical references and index.
Summary: "Describes SWAT teams operating in the United States, including their history, gear,
weapons, training, and missions"—Provided by publisher.
Audience: For children ages 8-13.
ISBN 978-1-4765-0112-3 (library binding)
ISBN 978-1-4765-3586-9 (ebook PDF)
1. Police—Special weapons and tactics units—United States—Juvenile literature.
2. Police training—United States—Juvenile literature. I. Title.
HV8080.S64G73 2014
363.2'3—dc23   2012045246

Editorial Credits
Carrie Braulick Sheely, editor; Bobbie Nuytten, designer; Laura Manthe, production specialist

Photo Credits
Alamy: Chuck Eckert, 6 (left), Ernesto Burciaga, 6 (right), JHP Public Safety, 42, Jochen
Tack, 32, Mikael Karlsson, 11, ZUMA Press, Inc., 44, ZUMA Wire Service, 27, 41; AP Images:
Mike Meadows, 19, Vince Bucci, 18; Corbis: Bettmann, 17, Dallas Morning News/Tom Fox,
39 (bottom), Sygma/Claude Salhani, 15, ZUMA Press/Courtney Sacco, 13; Dreamstime:
Andrey Kiselev, 35, Gregory Perkins, 31, Martin Brayley, 34; Indiana National Guard photo,
24; iStockphotos: Vesna Andjic, 9; Newscom: ZUMA Press/Hans Gutknecht, 7; Shutterstock:
cynoclub, 26 (top left, right), Dave Navarro Jr, 29, Digital Storm, 11, 23, 33, 42, 45 (silhouettes),
Dumitrescu Ciprian-Florin, 45, Eric Isselee, 26 (bottom left), Feng Yu, 18, Katarzyna
Mazurowska, cover, 30, Kbiros, 37 (middle, bottom), Marsan, 39 (top), PinkBlue, 37 (top),
Vudhikrai, 36 (bottom), zimand, 36 (top, middle); U.S. Air Force photo by Justin Connaher, 21,
Kemberly Groue, 20; U.S. Navy Photo by MC2 Maebel Tinoko, 25, MC2 Tucker M. Yates, 22, MC3
Kristopher Kirsop, 5

Artistic Effects
Shutterstock

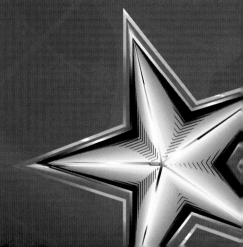

Printed in the United States of America in
North Mankato, Minnesota
032013   007223CGF13

TABLE of CONTENTS

DANGEROUS WORK

On January 10, 2013, employees were closing a department store in Los Angeles, California. Without warning, two armed men ran into the store and took them as hostages.

The Los Angeles SWAT team was called to the scene. Team members quickly surrounded the crime scene. After about three hours, they rushed into the store and rescued the 14 hostages. But the suspects managed to escape after robbing the store. They were arrested three days later.

Fact

SWAT teams are sometimes given other names, such as tactical response teams or tactical response units. But they basically operate the same way and conduct the same types of missions.

Being a member of a SWAT team is one of the most dangerous jobs in law enforcement. Only the most committed, most experienced, and most decisive officers are chosen as members.

On any given day, SWAT members may be called on to conduct dangerous missions. These missions may range from hostage rescue to **counterterrorism** operations. SWAT members might be involved in high-speed chases. They might have to pull wounded officers and civilians out of harm's way while under gunfire. No matter what their missions are, SWAT teams come prepared.

SWAT team members train to stay prepared for their dangerous missions.

hostage—a person held against his or her will
counterterrorism—actions taken against terrorism; terrorism is the use of violence and destructive acts to create fear and to achieve a political or religious goal

SWAT UNITS: ROLL CALL

SWAT teams operate on many levels, from local to federal. But they all have one thing in common—they are ready to respond to a crisis at a moment's notice.

MUNICIPAL:

Police departments in large cities throughout the United States have their own SWAT teams. These cities include New York, Chicago, and Los Angeles. Some mid-size cities also have their own SWAT teams.

REGIONAL:

Some small towns and cities pool their resources to form a regional SWAT team. A regional SWAT team usually serves several counties. Members of the teams come from police departments throughout the region. The Southwest Washington Regional SWAT team is one example.

COUNTY:

Some counties have many very small towns. In these cases, a SWAT team may operate out of a county law enforcement agency, such as a Sheriff's department.

STATE:

Most state police departments have their own SWAT units. These squads sometimes back up local SWAT teams.

NATIONAL:

Some countries organize SWAT teams on a national level. Countries with their own SWAT units include Finland, Argentina, the United Kingdom, Israel, and China. A national SWAT team serves as the first line of defense against acts of terrorism within a country's borders.

FEDERAL AGENCIES:

Several U.S. federal agencies have SWAT teams. These agencies include the Federal Bureau of Investigation (FBI), the Drug Enforcement Administration (DEA), and the U.S. Marshals Service. These units may be called in when certain federal laws are broken or when national security is threatened.

Fact

Ninety percent of U.S. cities with a population of 50,000 or more have SWAT teams.

7

Hostage and Barricade

On the morning of May 16, 2010, Jose Benitez was chasing three men who had just robbed him in his SUV. The robbery occurred on a residential street in Chelsea, Massachusetts. The three **suspects** panicked. They invaded a home, taking a family hostage. The suspects then **barricaded** themselves inside. The suspects soon released the family, but remained inside the house.

The SWAT team from nearby Boston was called to the scene. SWAT **negotiators** made contact with the suspects. After intense negotiations, the suspects surrendered over the course of about four hours. The negotiators' patience and hard work brought a peaceful end to the crisis.

Hostage and barricade situations are some of the most stressful events for SWAT teams. Innocent lives may be lost if the wrong move is made.

Hostage situations can occur in one of many situations. Family arguments can lead to hostage crises. Hostage situations may also break out as a result of workplace issues. The most common workplace hostage incidents involve employees who feel they have been wrongfully fired or demoted. Terrorists may take hostages to bring attention to their political goals or demands.

If negotiations fail, SWAT teams may decide to make an assault on a location. During a hostage or barricade situation, assaults are particularly dangerous.

suspect—someone thought to have committed a crime

barricade—to block a person's access by using a wall or other type of barrier to cause a separation; suspects often barricade themselves inside buildings

negotiator—a SWAT member who is trained to discuss matters with a suspect to arrive at a peaceful solution

High-Risk Warrants

Serving a routine **felony warrant** in Texas turned deadly on June 5, 2012. The suspect, 23-year-old Alexander Coan, was wanted for committing robbery. The Fort Worth city police and the Arlington city SWAT team tracked him to his Arlington apartment. Coan was in the apartment with his girlfriend. But there was a twist. Upon arriving, police realized that the pair was also holding a hostage who was an acquaintance of the couple.

Coan fired at the officers and shot Arlington SWAT member Bryan Graham in the head. An exchange of gunfire followed between Coan and police, and Coan was shot and killed. The SWAT team then freed the hostage. Graham recovered from his wound. Coan's girlfriend was arrested for kidnapping.

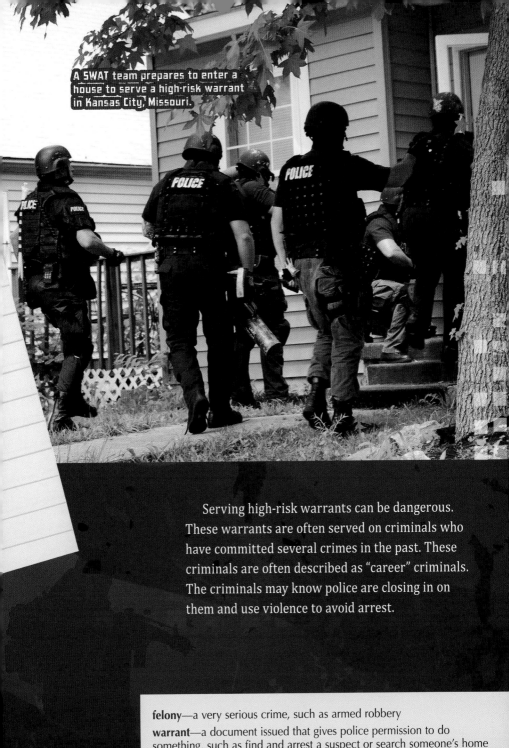

A SWAT team prepares to enter a house to serve a high-risk warrant in Kansas City, Missouri.

Serving high-risk warrants can be dangerous. These warrants are often served on criminals who have committed several crimes in the past. These criminals are often described as "career" criminals. The criminals may know police are closing in on them and use violence to avoid arrest.

felony—a very serious crime, such as armed robbery
warrant—a document issued that gives police permission to do something, such as find and arrest a suspect or search someone's home

Crowd Control and Civil Order

Thousands of people **protested** at a **NATO** meeting in Chicago, Illinois, in May 2012. Chicago SWAT team members were among the officers there to keep order. Even before the meeting began, plans were in place to handle the crowds. Police wanted to keep the anti-NATO protests from turning into **riots**. Some people who had threatened to harm public officials attending the meeting were taken into custody days before it began. In all, 91 people were arrested during the protests.

Police work to control the anti-NATO protests in Chicago in May 2012.

SWAT teams are often called in when large crowds gather. Like during other missions, SWAT members need to be well-disciplined and even-tempered during crowd control duties. Staying calm can help keep others from becoming angry. SWAT members need to maintain a strong but nonaggressive presence. If arrests need to be made, SWAT members close in on the suspects and quickly remove them.

Gorilla on the Loose

SWAT teams never know what their next call will bring. A 400-pound (181-kilogram) gorilla in the Buffalo, New York, zoo escaped from his cage on March 19, 2012. The Buffalo SWAT team was called in to handle the situation. The SWAT team kept zoo visitors safe by gathering them into a secure indoor location. Meanwhile, zookeepers used a tranquilizer dart to capture the ape.

protest—to object to something strongly and publicly

NATO—North Atlantic Treaty Organization; NATO includes countries from North America and Europe that have formed an alliance to help maintain peace and defend one another

riot—a large gathering of people who use violence to show their anger

Terrorism

In October 1977 passengers of Lufthansa Flight 181 calmly boarded their plane on the Spanish island of Mallorca. They were bound for Germany. They had no reason to suspect anything was wrong. But the passengers would soon fear for their lives. Four terrorists hijacked the flight. They **diverted** the flight and demanded that terrorists being held in a German prison be freed. When the plane stopped in Yemen to refuel, the terrorists killed the plane's pilot.

The German federal SWAT team, known as GSG 9, responded to the hijacking. Eventually, the copilot landed the plane in Mogadishu, Somalia, in Africa. GSG 9 members had arrived at the airport before the plane landed. While one SWAT officer negotiated with the terrorists, fellow GSG 9 members stormed the plane. They killed three of the terrorists and wounded the fourth. The 86 passengers and remaining crew members were freed.

Reacting to terrorist attacks is especially dangerous for SWAT teams. Terrorists are usually heavily armed with a variety of weapons. They could have high-powered guns or deadly explosives. Terrorists may set booby traps in areas around the main crime scene. Some terrorists are not afraid to die for their cause. These dangerous criminals use violence without fear of an attack from police.

SWAT teams know that terrorists can quickly turn violent. SWAT officers surround the area quickly and prepare to move in with force.

SWAT teams are sometimes called in when even a small sign signals a possible terrorist attack. For example, a SWAT team might be called if someone leaves a suitcase unattended at an airport. First, the SWAT team would **evacuate** everyone from the scene. Then the team would investigate to find out if any danger is present.

Fact

Many national SWAT teams have names of animals that are known for their hunting abilities. These names include the Helsinki (Finland) Bears, the Argentina Hawks, and the Snow Leopard Commando Unit of China.

The Lufthansa Flight 181 hijackers landed in several places before arriving in Mogadishu, including Dubai (shown). GSG 9 members were planning to assault the plane there, but the plane took off before they could.

divert—to change from one course to another
evacuate—to leave a dangerous place and go somewhere safer

MAKING HISTORY

SWAT teams first began organizing in the mid-1960s. Police realized that criminals were arming themselves with better weaponry and more carefully planning crimes. One particular event in the United States made these facts clearer than ever before.

A Tragic Event

Shots rang out from the clock tower on the University of Texas campus in Austin on August 1, 1966. Charles Whitman was up in the tower's 28th floor, firing guns at fellow students.

The Austin police had no weapons that could match Whitman's sawed-off shotgun and three rifles. He fired for just over 90 minutes. Eventually, two Austin police officers quietly climbed up the tower. Confronting Whitman, they killed him in a shoot-out. Fourteen people died after being shot by Whitman, and 31 were wounded.

The tragic event sent a clear message to law enforcement agencies around the country—specially equipped police forces were needed. Los Angeles police officer John Nelson knew a large city might face a similar situation. He asked his police department to establish a special emergency response team. In 1967 this team became the nation's first SWAT unit. Officials in other U.S. cities soon organized their own teams.

SWAT Teams Start Around the World

An event in Germany prompted countries and cities around the world to establish SWAT teams. Terrorism erupted during the 1972 Olympic Games in the city of Munich. A Palestinian terrorist group called Black September invaded the living quarters of the Israeli Olympic team. The eight terrorists killed one Israeli athlete and a coach. They also took nine hostages.

As in the Texas tower shooting, police didn't have adequate firepower. They had undergone no special training to deal with this kind of situation. After a 21-hour standoff, Munich city police launched a failed rescue attempt. It resulted in the death of all the hostages.

Gun smoke clouds the area in front of Whitman's position in the University of Texas clock tower on August 1, 1966.

SWAT TEAMS IN THE HEADLINES

U.S. SWAT teams have a long history of bravery under fire. They have answered hundreds of thousands of calls. Here are just a few stories that made major headlines.

SWAT Team Brings Shooting Spree to End

SAN DIEGO, CA JULY 18, 1984

Armed with numerous weapons, James Oliver Huberty walked into a McDonald's restaurant in San Diego on July 18, 1984. He killed 21 people and wounded 19 more. The San Diego SWAT team responded. A SWAT officer on the roof of a neighboring building took aim at Huberty and fired. The shot killed Huberty before he could shoot more people in the restaurant.

SWAT Team Saves Hostage after Attempted Bank Robbery

PORTLAND, OR APRIL 13, 1991 — SWAT members brought an end to a daring bank robbery attempt in Oregon on April 13, 1991. Michael Lee Henry ordered a teller at the Pacific First Bank in Portland to give him all her cash. Before she could do that, he jumped over the counter and took her and another teller hostage. Henry forced the hostages into a back room. The Portland SWAT team feared that the robber would harm the hostages and staged an assault. When SWAT members entered the back room, Henry dragged one of the hostages into a closet with him. The SWAT members then tossed a flash bang into the closet. This device gives off a burst of light and a loud noise. When the weapon went off, the hostage dropped to the floor and crawled out of the closet. When Henry pointed his gun at the hostage, SWAT officers shot and killed him.

17 Wounded After Bank Robbery Attempt

LOS ANGELES, CA FEB. 28, 1997 — Emil Matasareanu and Larry Phillips Jr. were heavily armed and wearing body armor. They tried to rob a North Hollywood Bank of America branch on February 28, 1997. Los Angeles police officers surrounded the bank, but their weapons were no match for the robbers'. The Los Angeles SWAT team was called to the scene. Later the suspects came out firing. SWAT members and other police officers fired back. The incident left 11 police officers and six civilians wounded. The two bank robbers died in the shoot-out.

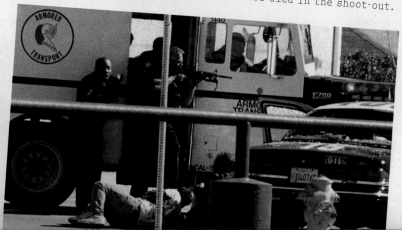

Chapter 3

TAKING UP POSITIONS

Each SWAT unit works as a team. Each team member has a job, and each job has to be done precisely as planned.

Commander:

The commander is in charge of the entire SWAT operation. This person develops the strategy and decides on the **tactical deployment** of all team members.

Scouts:

Scouts gather information before an entry team goes in to make an assault. They gather this information by talking to witnesses, studying the scene, and using high-tech equipment.

Rear Guard:

This is the last person in a SWAT formation. The rear guard makes sure no one sneaks up behind the team. Often walking backward, the rear guard checks out the area, looking for any surprise attackers.

Assault/Entry Team:

These officers rush the scene if a forced entry is ordered.

Pointman/ Pointwoman

This person leads the entry team from its hidden area to the target. He or she is the first person to confront any danger along the way.

Negotiators:

Negotiators make one-on-one contact with the suspect. They try to talk the suspect out of committing any violence. In most cases, the negotiator is one of the most experienced SWAT team members but never the commander.

Spotters:

Spotters stay alongside the snipers. The spotters assist the snipers if the order is given to shoot a suspect. Spotters are equipped with high-powered binoculars. These officers identify targets, estimate distances, and help snipers establish a clear line of fire.

Snipers:

With powerful rifles, these sharpshooters usually take positions on the rooftop of a high building near the crime scene. They are prepared to shoot if the order is given.

tactical deployment—positioning of the members of a team in the best way possible

SELECTION PROCESS

The announcement has been posted: there is an opening on the SWAT team. Police look for experienced officers with outstanding performance for the SWAT unit. They also want people who work well as part of a team. However, SWAT units do not generally actively seek out officers for their teams. Those who want to be on SWAT teams volunteer for the job.

Generally, a selection board of three to five experienced officers reviews the personnel records of SWAT candidates. Each candidate is interviewed before a selection is made.

Among the traits that make a valued SWAT team member are:

⊕ Good decision-making skills:

SWAT members must be able to take quick, decisive action and make quick assessments of crisis situations. They may need to think of creative ways to solve problems.

⊕ Emotional stability:

SWAT members must be able to remain calm when dealing with suspects.

⊕ Quick reflexes:

SWAT members must respond quickly as situations change.

⊕ Physical fitness:

SWAT members have to be physically fit. They may need to quickly carry victims to safety or move heavy equipment.

⊕ Good skills with weaponry:

SWAT members have to be able to expertly handle firearms.

Fact

SWAT teams throughout the United States respond to about 40,000 calls each year.

STAYING READY

Being prepared is key to the success of any SWAT mission. It can mean the difference between life and death for team members and civilians.

SWAT members train to stay prepared for calls. Individual SWAT members maintain their own physical fitness routines. Members also train together as a team. For example, each SWAT member of the city of Tampa, Florida, is required to train 270 hours each year.

Many police departments use realistic SWAT situations and add new twists for their training sessions. For example, equipment failures may be part of a session. Some SWAT teams ask local college drama students to play roles. These students help make the training scenarios more realistic.

Units train during the day, at night, and in all weather conditions. Team members are in full uniform and fully equipped. Their weapons have blank **cartridges**. These cartridges have no bullets. However, they still make an explosive sound and flash.

Training sessions are usually recorded on video cameras. Police officials watch the recordings. The officials see where SWAT members perform well and where they need to improve.

cartridge—a container holding the gunpowder, primer, and ammunition for a gun

K·9 SWAT MEMBERS

Some SWAT members aren't human—they're canines. Just like human SWAT members, dogs on the squad must be brave, strong, intelligent, and quick. The breeds most often recruited by SWAT teams are Belgian Malinois, Dutch Shepherds, and German Shepherds. These breeds are known for their intelligence, courage, and trainability. SWAT canines are considered so valuable that each one wears a custom-made bulletproof vest.

SWAT K-9s have many responsibilities. They may patrol outer **perimeters** of a crime scene or capture a fleeing suspect. They may enter areas of a building that a person cannot fit into. Some SWAT canines are trained as bomb-sniffing dogs. These dogs alert the team if a suspect has planted explosives.

Belgian Malinois

Dutch Shepherd

German Shepherd

Generally, a dog works with one handler. But all SWAT members of a unit train with the dog. This cross-team training makes it possible for the dog to work with any team member in an emergency.

In many SWAT missions, a dog must remain silent. Barking could let a suspect know that the SWAT unit is nearby. Dogs must learn to recognize orders in the form of hand signals. This ability helps ensure a silent, surprise entry for the SWAT team.

A SWAT member and his dog respond to a barricade situation in Aliso Viejo, California.

Fact

Dogs are very useful on night missions. They have excellent vision and hearing. These sharp senses allow dogs to pick up sounds and movements their human handlers cannot.

perimeter—a border or edge

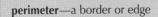

Chapter 4

MOVING IN

Criminals can strike anywhere. SWAT teams must be able to reach crime scenes by land, air, or sea. They also need specially equipped vehicles for their dangerous missions.

Trucks

Most SWAT teams use large armored trucks. These trucks transport SWAT officers and provide cover. Some SWAT trucks are modified buses or vans. Other SWAT trucks are custom-built.

SWAT trucks carry a variety of equipment. This equipment often includes:

a breaching hook
a large metal hook used to rip bars from windows and doors

a battering ram
a long steel cylindrical tool used to break down doors

a Hooligan tool
a large tool with a flattened blade on one side and an ax on the other; used to pry open a door

ladders
to help SWAT members launch an assault on tall buildings by climbing through windows

grappling hooks and rope
to help SWAT members rappel down the sides of buildings

A few units purchase **decommissioned** military tanks and turn them into SWAT vehicles. These heavy-duty vehicles can knock down doors and walls.

Fact

Some of the newest SWAT vehicles are modeled after U.S. military trucks such as armored troop carriers.

rappel—to go down the side of a building using a rope
decommission—to take out of service

Helicopters

A helicopter is a big advantage for any SWAT unit. It allows the team to gather **intelligence** from the air. During vehicle pursuits, SWAT members in helicopters can provide moment-by-moment scene updates to ground units.

Helicopters can also land SWAT members in key positions. They are especially useful when the crime scene is in a tall building. In that case, helicopters can carry SWAT officers to the building's roof. From there, the SWAT members can rappel down the building to gain entry. Helicopters carry SWAT snipers to rooftops as well.

Helicopters are even helpful for creating diversions because they are noisy. Suspects often lose their concentration when they hear a helicopter approaching. It can be easier for a SWAT unit on the ground to make a surprise entry if a suspect is distracted.

Helicopters are sometimes equipped with large metal buckets hanging from a cable. These buckets can bring equipment to SWAT officers on a rooftop. They may also carry rescued hostages or officers from rooftops.

intelligence—information about an enemy's plans or actions

Boats

Many SWAT teams—especially those based near oceans and large bodies of water—have several boats. These boats range from 25-foot (7.6-meter) inflatable rafts and speedboats to 72-foot (22-m) armored boats. Like SWAT trucks, SWAT boats are well-equipped with tools and weapons.

Boats are useful to SWAT teams in many ways. Sometimes a SWAT unit responds to an incident taking place in a building facing water. To set up a perimeter, the SWAT team uses watercraft to fully surround the site. SWAT officers in boats can pursue suspects fleeing on the water. They can also search for suspects holding hostages on watercraft.

Danger at Sea

Missions on water can be tricky, especially if criminals are on large metal ships. Bullets may ricochet off the ship's side and come back to hit a SWAT member. In addition, suspects can hide in secure areas below the main deck and behind heavy metal doors.

Fact

U.S. cities with SWAT boats include New York; Nashville, Tennessee; Santa Barbara, California; and Seattle, Washington.

ricochet—to bounce off a solid surface and go in another direction

Chapter 5

ARMED AND READY

The right tools and vehicles are just two factors important to a SWAT mission's success. Teams need high-powered weapons and protective safety gear as well.

Suit Up

SWAT members are covered in protective gear from head to toe. Each piece plays an important role in keeping a team member safe.

GOGGLES: Goggles protect the eyes from sand, dust, glass fragments, and caustic liquids that might be thrown at a SWAT officer. Special night-vision goggles help officers see in the dark. These goggles magnify available light and can make dim images 100 times clearer.

BODY ARMOR: Once referred to as a bulletproof vest, this protective garment is now called body armor. It fits on the upper part of the body and protects the vital organs, including the heart and lungs. Body armor can be worn underneath the outer clothing. It can also be placed in a nylon raid cover that is worn over the clothing. Body armor is lightweight and made of a strong tightly woven material called Kevlar. Kevlar is five times stronger than steel. Body armor deflects bullets, but some knives can go through it.

POLICE

BALLISTIC HELMET: Similar to a military helmet, the ballistic helmet shields the head from injury. It provides protection from bullets, falls, and hard hits by objects.

BALACLAVA: Worn under the helmet, a balaclava is similar to a ski mask. It is fire-resistant and protects the officer from flying glass, harsh chemicals, sparks, fire, and smoke. By covering the nose and mouth, the balaclava reduces the amount of smoke and fumes the officer breathes in.

JUMPSUIT: Some SWAT members wear one-piece, dark-colored jumpsuits. Others wear military battle uniforms. Both types of uniforms are made of fire-resistant rayon. This material is flexible yet very strong.

GLOVES: SWAT members wear gloves made of a strong, fire-resistant material called Nomex. These gloves protect the hands from heat and provide good grip.

BALLISTIC SHIELD: This handheld shield is made of a heavy-duty plastic called polyethylene. It defends against bullets.

caustic—extremely harsh and capable of causing harm; chemicals that burn the skin are caustic

WEAPONS

SWAT teams are equipped with a large range of weapons. Each weapon is chosen specifically to complete a certain mission. Having a large variety helps ensure that SWAT teams can match weapons to the tasks they face.

LETHAL WEAPONS

Semiautomatic Handguns:
SWAT officers carry semiautomatic pistols, such as Glocks. These rapid-fire handguns are easier to reload than standard handguns.

Rifles:
SWAT teams use a variety of long-range rifles. Many teams use modified hunting rifles, such as a bolt-action .243 Winchester. SWAT snipers practice shooting their rifles at targets up to 0.5 mile (0.8 km) away.

Shotguns:
Shotguns are easy to handle and work best at close range. Shotguns can be loaded with less lethal rounds, such as rock-salt shells or rubber bullets. SWAT teams often use rock-salt shells or rubber bullets to control riots.

Submachine Guns:
Submachine guns are accurate, compact, and reliable. They can be set to fire either a single shot or several shots automatically in rapid-fire bursts. Among the most common models is the Heckler & Koch (HK) MP5 9 mm.

LESS LETHAL WEAPONS

Sting Grenades:
Small, hard rubber balls fly out of a sting grenade. They sting like a swarm of hornets. Sting grenades often disable a suspect.

Flash bangs:
Flash bangs are explosive devices that produce a blinding flash of light and a loud noise. They are designed to confuse or distract suspects.

Stun Guns:
Stun guns are handheld devices that use electroshock to disable suspects. The gun is pressed against the suspect. At the push of a button, an electrical charge fires across the front of the gun and into the suspect. This charge temporarily disables the suspect by interfering with muscle function.

Taser Guns:
Taser guns work similarly to stun guns. But they can be used on a suspect from a greater distance than stun guns. When the trigger is pulled, wires fly out of the gun. Barbs are connected to the wires, which attach to the suspect's clothing. Once the barbs are attached, the electrical charge travels through the wires and into the body.

Tear gas:
Tear-gas canisters release a harsh chemical. The chemical causes pain in the eyes, nose, mouth, and lungs. It can even cause temporary blindness.

Chapter 6

TACTICS

Gathering Intelligence

Data is one of a SWAT team's best weapons. Gathering intelligence gives the team the facts it needs to make a strategy. All intelligence is sent to the SWAT team's command post. Officers there study intelligence and update plans accordingly. The command post can be set up in a SWAT vehicle, in a nearby building, or even in a large tent.

Intelligence includes all information available, such as:

- ➔ the suspects' identities
- ➔ how much firepower the suspects have
- ➔ whether there are any hostages
- ➔ possible escape routes

SWAT officers gather some intelligence by closely observing the scene. The team picks up other information by talking to witnesses. Team members may also study historical records such as building plans. SWAT members in helicopters may take aerial photos and video. Snipers can gather information by using their scopes.

Some units have high-tech intelligence-gathering tools. Small cameras might be slipped through a crack in a window or ceiling. The cameras can stream video back to the command post. Through the same methods, SWAT officers can slide microphones into buildings to hear what is happening.

Robots on the Scene

Long used by bomb squads, robots are one of the newest tools used by SWAT teams. Equipped with cameras, robots can get close to a crime scene and send back images of what is happening. Robots can also bring food and other supplies to hostage-takers. SWAT officers then do not need to put themselves at risk.

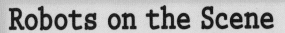

SECURING THE PERIMETERS

When a SWAT team first arrives at a scene, securing the inner and outer perimeters is the number-one priority. This process limits the criminal activity to one area. In a hostage situation, securing the perimeters prevents more hostages from being taken. If someone is shooting from behind a barricade, clearing the perimeter prevents bystanders from being shot. The perimeters are not left unguarded at any time.

INNER PERIMETER

The inner perimeter is an area of extreme danger. SWAT officers make the inner perimeter as tight around the scene as possible. Once the SWAT team sets up an inner perimeter, the suspects have no clear escape route.

SWAT team members stationed at the inner perimeter carry more lethal weapons than those at the outer perimeter. These SWAT members are dressed in full gear and are ready to launch an assault.

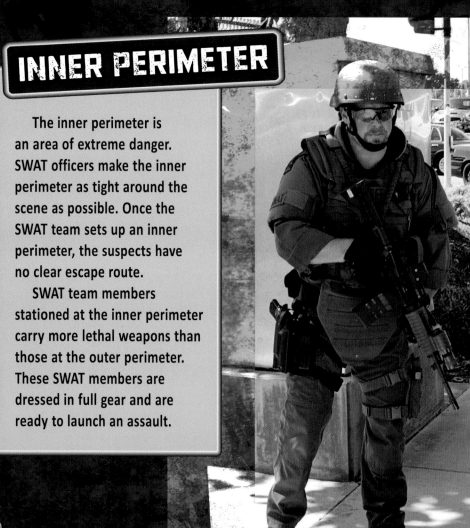

OUTER PERIMETER

At the outer perimeter, there is less danger. Here spectators such as the news media can stand in relative safety. SWAT officers secure the outer perimeter to make sure that no one wanders into the danger zone.

A SWAT team member guards his perimeter at a crime scene in San Clemente California, in September 2011.

ENDING A STANDOFF

A SWAT team arrives and secures the area. The suspect makes demands and refuses to surrender. The situation has reached a standoff.

The first step toward ending a standoff is having the SWAT negotiator contact the suspect. The contact is usually made by phone. This method helps the negotiator establish a relationship with the suspect.

The negotiator does everything possible not to anger the suspect. Time is very valuable to the negotiator. The goal is to wear down the suspect. The negotiator works to convince a suspect that there is no way out other than surrendering. Along the way, the negotiator may make deals with the suspect for small items. For example, the negotiator may agree to bring food and water to the suspect.

Trojan Horse Assault

SWAT teams may try a Trojan horse assault before making a regular assault. Using this strategy, an officer dressed as a civilian does something nonthreatening, like delivers food. Then the officer tries to quickly take down the suspect.

This type of assault gets its name from an ancient Greek legend. According to the legend, the Greeks built a large wooden horse to invade the city of Troy. The Greeks had been fighting the Trojans in a long war. The Greeks offered the horse as a gift to the Trojans. The Trojans brought the horse into their city. Soon afterward, Greek soldiers who had been hiding inside the horse snuck out. They defeated the Trojans, ending the war.

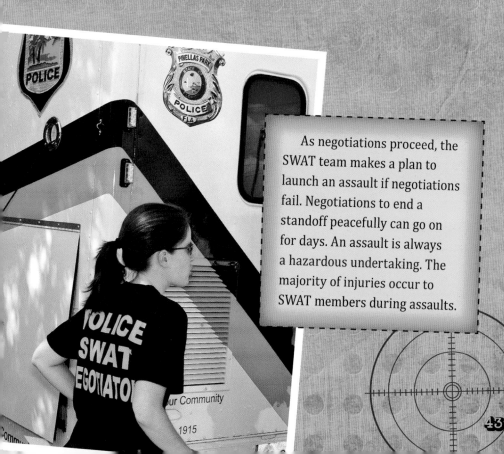

As negotiations proceed, the SWAT team makes a plan to launch an assault if negotiations fail. Negotiations to end a standoff peacefully can go on for days. An assault is always a hazardous undertaking. The majority of injuries occur to SWAT members during assaults.

WORKING TOGETHER

For some missions, SWAT teams call in other specialized
emergency units. SWAT teams train with many of these uni[...]
the groups are prepared to work together.

Paramedic units are commonly called [...]
scenes. Paramedics are trained to provid[...]
SWAT team members and victims at the [...]

If a suspect has dangerous liquids, gases, or other h[...]
materials, SWAT teams call in a hazardous materials ([...]
team. HazMat officers understand the dangers of the[...]
materials. They know how to safely remove them or c[...]
them if they are released. These officers also know ho[...]
people who have been exposed to the materials.

A bomb squad responds to a call.

At the first sign that explosives may be present, SWAT teams call in a bomb squad. Bomb squads are trained to identify and disarm explosive devices. Bomb squads also develop plans to handle explosives.

SWAT teams stand ready for action at a moment's notice. These courageous officers put their lives at risk to save the lives of others day in and day out.

GLOSSARY

barricade (BA-ruh-kade)—to block a person's access by using a wall or other type of barrier to cause a separation

cartridge (KAHR-trij)—a container holding a gun's powder, primer, and bullet

caustic (KOS-tik)—able to destroy or eat away by chemical action

counterterrorism (KOWN-tur-ter-ur-i-zuhm)—actions taken against terrorism; terrorism is the use of violence and destructive acts to create fear and to achieve a political or religious goal

decommission (dee-kuh-MI-shuhn)—to take out of service

divert (dih-VERT)—to change from one course to another

evacuate (i-VA-kyuh-wayt)— to leave an area during a time of danger

felony (FEL-uhn-ee)—a very serious crime, usually punishable by imprisonment

hostage (HOSS-tij)—a person held against his or her will

intelligence (in-TEL-uh-jenss)—information about an enemy's plans or actions

NATO (NAY-toh)—North Atlantic Treaty Organization; NATO includes countries from North America and Europe that have formed an alliance to help maintain peace and defend one another

negotiator (ni-GOH-shee-ay-tor)—a person trained to handle a matter through discussion and compromise rather than force

perimeter (puh-RIM-uh-tur)—the outer edge or boundary of an area

protest (pro-TEST)—to object to something strongly and publicly

rappel (ruh-PEL)—to slide down a strong rope

ricochet (RIK-uh-shay)—to hit a hard surface and go in a different direction

riot (RYE-uht)—a large gathering of people who use violence to show their anger

suspect (SUHSS-pekt)—someone thought to be responsible for a crime

tactical deployment (TAK-ti-kuhl di-PLOI-muhnt)—the positioning of the members of a team in the best way possible

warrant (WOR-uhnt)—a document issued that gives police permission to do something, such as find and arrest a suspect or search someone's home

READ MORE

Gagne, Tammy. *Police Dogs.* Dogs on the Job. North Mankato, Minn.: Capstone, 2014.

Ollhoff, Jim. *Swat.* Emergency Workers. Minneapolis: ABDO Pub. Co, 2012.

Tisdale, Rachel. *Police Officers.* The World's Most Dangerous Jobs. New York: Crabtree Pub. Co., 2012.

White, Nancy. *Police Officers to the Rescue.* The Work of Heroes: First Responders in Action. New York: Bearport Pub., 2012.

INTERNET SITES

FactHound offers a safe, fun way to find Internet sites related to this book. All of the sites on FactHound have been researched by our staff.

Here's all you do:

Visit www.facthound.com

Type in this code: 9781476501123

www.FACTHOUND.com

INDEX